Anything is POSSIBLE

Inspiring true stories for tween girls about courage, dreaming big, and never giving up.

TWEEN SUCCESS

This book belongs to:

SOMETHING
FOR YOU

Get your <u>FREE</u> Printable Workbook!

To download your free workbook

Table of Contents

It all starts here...

I've got a secret to share with you... a secret that will change your life. This secret has the power to make all your dreams come true. It's the key to success, happiness, and a bright future.

The secret is simple: ANYTHING IS POSSIBLE.

Yes, anything. You can be whoever you want to be, do whatever you dream of doing, and achieve anything you set your mind to. Just imagine what you could do if you genuinely believed anything was possible.

IT'S ALL ABOUT HAVING THE COURAGE TO PURSUE YOUR DREAMS, THE SELF-BELIEF TO KNOW THAT YOU CAN ACHIEVE THEM, AND THE PERSEVERANCE TO KEEP GOING WHEN THINGS GET TOUGH.

This book will explore what it means to dream big and work hard and how having the right mindset is the key to a successful life. We'll meet inspiring people who have overcome failure to achieve their goals and learn that failure is part of success.

Some of the people we'll meet you might already have heard of. Others, you'll learn about for the first time. But they all have one thing in common: They refused to give up on their dreams, no matter what.

Take Kalpana Chawla, for example. Kalpana dreamed of becoming an astronaut but was told it was impossible. She didn't give up, though. She worked hard and achieved her dream of becoming the first Indian American woman in space.

Or what about Malala Yousafzai? When she was just a teenager, Malala was shot for speaking out against the treatment of girls and women. She could have given up then, but she recovered and continued her fight for education, becoming the youngest Nobel Prize laureate.

We'll also meet:
- A girl who was told she would never walk again, but went on to become an Olympic champion.

- A writer who was rejected 12 times before she landed a publisher. (Spoiler alert: She went on to sell over 500 million copies of her books! Guess those rejections didn't matter so much after all.

- A surfer who lost her arm in a shark attack but got back on her board a month later and is now one of the best pro surfers in the world.

These stories will show you that anyone can achieve great things, no matter who they are or where they come from. At the end of each chapter, we'll explore the themes more in-depth with fun activities based on the topics.

But before we begin, there's one more thing....

THIS IS YOUR BOOK.

Yes, yours.

MAKE IT WHATEVER YOU WANT IT TO BE.

So go ahead — color outside the lines, write in the margins, and add your own stories and illustrations. This book is for you, and it's meant to be used however you see fit.

Now let's get started on this journey together. Are you ready?

ANYTHING IS POSSIBLE!

It always seems

IMPOSSIBLE

UNTIL it's

DONE.

- Nelson Mandela

Chapter 1

COURAGE & THE POWER OF POSITIVE THINKING

All our **DREAMS** CAN **COME TRUE** if we have the **COURAGE** to **PURSUE** them.

- Walt Disney

When faced with a challenge, it's easy to give up and think it's too hard. But anything is possible if you have courage and a positive attitude. Let's explore this further.

What is courage?

The dictionary defines courage as "the ability to do something that frightens one; bravery."

But what does that really mean?

Being courageous doesn't mean that you're never scared. It's normal to feel afraid when you're facing a challenge. For example, you might be scared to sing or give a speech on stage.

Courage means that you don't let your fear stop you.

THE ONLY WAY TO OVERCOME YOUR FEAR IS TO FACE IT HEAD-ON. TAKE A DEEP BREATH, STEP OUT OF YOUR COMFORT ZONE, AND DO IT ANYWAY.

Now let's look at the power of positive thinking.

What is positive thinking?

POSITIVE THINKING
IS HAVING A POSITIVE ATTITUDE AND
BELIEVING IN YOURSELF.

It's knowing that you can achieve anything you set your mind to, even when the odds seem against you.

For example, if you're trying to learn a new skill and keep getting frustrated because you can't seem to get it right, a positive thinker would see this as an opportunity to learn and grow. They wouldn't give up because they know they will eventually get it if they keep trying.

Let's put these two concepts together and meet some people who have used courage and positive thinking to achieve amazing things.

Malala Yousafzai

EDUCATION ACTIVIST (1997 – PRESENT)

Malala Yousafzai is a Pakistani activist who campaigns for the rights of girls to learn. She is the
youngest person to receive the Nobel Peace Prize.

⸴I am STRONGER than fear. ⸴

— Malala Yousafzai

Imagine being told you could never go to school or get an education — or that you could go to school, but you would be risking your life if you did. This was Malala Yousafzai's reality.

Malala was born on July 12, 1997, in Mingora, Pakistan. She came from a family that inspired girls to learn and credits her upbringing with her later activism. Her father was an activist who owned schools, wrote poetry, and, like his daughter, devoted his life to fighting for children's rights.

But Malala's education dreams were cut short when an extremist religious and political movement called the Taliban seized power in her home district of Swat and banned all girls from attending school.

Malala was not about to give up on her dreams. Despite the danger, she spoke publicly against the Taliban's policy of banning girls from attending school. In September 2009, at just 11 years of age and accompanied by her father, she gave her first speech, "How dare the Taliban take away my basic right to education?" This speech set Malala on a path that would change her life and have far-reaching consequences.

Around this time, the BBC approached Malala's father to find someone who would blog for them anonymously about what it was like to live under Taliban rule. Malala accepted the opportunity and began writing regularly for the BBC under the name Gul Makai.

However, all of this came at a price for Malala. It was not long before the Taliban discovered that Gul Makai was, in fact, Malala. The Taliban were now watching her every move.

In 2012, when Malala was 15, a masked Taliban gunman boarded her school bus, shouting, "Who is Malala?" and shot her in the head.

Miraculously, the bullet missed Malala's brain, and she survived. But she was in critical condition. Six days later, she was airlifted to England for treatment by a specialist. At first, her face was completely paralyzed from her wounds, but she gradually regained movement and sensation.

After a long and challenging recovery process that doctors said was "against the odds," Malala was reunited with her parents and well enough to leave the hospital.

While she was recovering, Malala's story made headlines all over the world. People were shocked that the Taliban targeted a young girl for speaking out about her right to education.

THE TALIBAN HAD TRIED TO SILENCE HER, BUT THEY MADE MALALA MORE DETERMINED THAN EVER TO KEEP FIGHTING FOR EDUCATION RIGHTS AND GIRLS' EMPOWERMENT.

In 2013, Malala addressed the United Nations and gave a speech calling for universal education. The same year, she published her first book, "I Am Malala."

At 17, MALALA BECAME THE FIRST AND ONLY CHILD TO RECEIVE THE NOBEL PEACE PRIZE.

This is an award that has been given to world leaders like Nelson Mandela and Martin Luther King Jr.

In the same year, she co-founded the Malala Fund, which provides grants to support local education initiatives for girls. Along the way, she met with then-US President Barack Obama. The UN dedicated a day to her, and Time named her among the world's 100 most influential people.

Malala's story inspires people worldwide, proving that anything is possible, no matter how difficult life may seem. Her courage and determination are an example to us all.

One PERSON CAN MAKE a big DIFFERENCE.

Bethany Hamilton

PRO SURFER (1990 – PRESENT)

Bethany Hamilton is a professional surfer who, despite losing her arm to a shark attack, continued to pursue her passion for surfing.

⋮ COURAGE

means you DON'T LET

fear STOP you. ⋮

- Bethany Hamilton

Think about the last time you were afraid to do something. Maybe you were afraid of failing or looking stupid in front of your friends. Whatever it was, you didn't do it because you were scared.

Bethany Hamilton knows a thing or two about fear. Her story is an excellent reminder that we should never let fear stop us from doing what we love.

Born on February 8, 1990, and raised in Hawaii, Bethany started surfing when she was three.

HER DREAM WAS TO ONE DAY BECOME A PROFESSIONAL SURFER.

At eight years old, she began competing in surfing competitions. Bethany's natural talent and dedication to practice saw her quickly rise through the ranks. By the time she was 10, she had her first sponsorship deal.

It seemed that everything was aligned for her to have a successful future in surfing. However, life doesn't always work out how we expect it to.

In 2003, Bethany's life took a dramatic turn. She was surfing with her friends off the coast of Kauai when she was attacked by a 14-foot tiger shark. Lying face down on her board with her left arm dangling in the water, Bethany was helpless as the shark attacked her and bit her arm.

Incredibly, with the help of her friends, Bethany managed to make it back to shore, where she received emergency treatment. However, her injuries were severe. The shark had bitten off her left arm, just below the shoulder.

Most people would have given up on their dreams at this point. The fear of going back into the water would have been too much to overcome. But Bethany is not like most people.

Despite the odds, she got back ON HER SURFBOARD just ONE MONTH AFTER THE SHARK ATTACK.

She went on to compete in numerous surfing competitions, and in 2007 she won her first national title. In 2010, Bethany made history by becoming the first one-armed surfer to win a major professional competition.

BETHANY IS A TRUE CHAMPION.

She continues to surf at the highest level and is an inspiration to people worldwide.

 She has appeared on numerous television shows, including Oprah, and in 2011 her story was made into a film titled "Soul Surfer."

Bethany's story is one of courage, determination, and resilience. It is an inspirational example of what it means to never give up on your dreams, no matter how hard life gets.

The next time you feel afraid of doing something, remember Bethany Hamilton and her courage in the face of adversity.

GO OUT THERE AND DO WHATEVER YOU'RE SCARED OF.

If Bethany can do it, so can you!

Jessica Watson

SAILOR (1997 – PRESENT)

Jessica Watson is an Australian sailor who, at 16 years of age, became the youngest person to sail solo, non-stop, and unassisted around the globe.

> ÷ **You** don't have
> to be someone **special**
> to **achieve**
> something **AMAZING.** ÷
>
> - **Jessica Watson**

Imagine being on a boat in the middle of the ocean, all alone, for 210 days — no land in sight, just you and the endless expanse of blue water, surviving on freeze-dried food and only sleeping for 20 minutes at a time.

For most of us, that would be a nightmare. But for Jessica Watson, it was a dream come true.

Born on May 18, 1997, on the Queensland Gold Coast in Australia, Jessica was a shy, quiet child. From the age of eight, she took sailing lessons with her brother and two sisters, and when she was 11, her family decided to live on a 52-foot cabin cruiser boat.

While being home-schooled, Jessica's yearning for adventure grew. Her mom read Jesse Martin's book "Lionheart" aloud to her at night. Jesse had sailed solo around the world at age 18, and Jessica was hooked, telling her mom she wanted to do the same thing.

By the age of 12, Jessica had made up her mind. She was going to sail around the world on her own and break Jesse's record as the youngest person to do so. But before she could set sail, Jessica had to prove that she was capable of such a journey. It took her four years of hard  work, logging over 12,000 miles of sailing experience, before she was ready to embark on her solo circumnavigation.

Finally, in 2009, she was ready, and her round-the-world trip was announced.

Her VOYAGE WOULD COVER NEARLY 23,000 NAUTICAL MILES AND WAS EXPECTED TO TAKE EIGHT MONTHS TO COMPLETE.

She planned to sail non-stop and unaided, which meant no other person could help her along the way except to give her advice via radio communication. But not everyone agreed with Jessica's decision to sail solo around the world at such a young age. Some people thought she was too inexperienced and that the journey was too dangerous. Jessica, however, was determined and continued planning for her trip.

Sometimes, things don't always turn out how we plan them. During a test run in September 2009, while sailing from Brisbane to Sydney, Jessica's 30-foot pink sailboat, "Ella's Pink Lady," accidentally collided with a 722-foot cargo ship in the early morning. Her boat's mast broke and the deck was damaged, but luckily Jessica man-  aged to gain control and return the sailboat to shore. Despite the danger, Jessica was determined. She would continue with her voyage once her yacht was repaired.

On October 18, Jessica's dream turned into reality as she set off on her adventure and sailed "Ella's Pink Lady" out of Sydney

Harbor. Her route would take her through some of the world's most dangerous waters and remote oceans. She would sail past northern New Zealand, Fiji, Samoa, South America, and South Africa before returning to Sydney, Australia. It would take all her courage, strength, and determination to finish the journey.

In January 2010, several days after passing the Falkland Islands in the Atlantic Ocean, the skies grew gray as Jessica sailed into a 12-hour-long, violent storm with hurricane-force winds.

HER BOAT CAPSIZED FOUR TIMES AS IT WAS TOSSED BY THE 32-FOOT-HIGH SWELLS

AND PLUNGED INTO THE OCEAN.

Luckily, her boat was designed to right itself if it capsized, and she was safely in the galley, out of immediate danger. Although "Ella's Pink Lady" was slightly damaged, Jessica remained positive and fixed the storm damage.

Just when she thought her trip was nearing its end, Jessica sailed into more dangerous weather south of Australia. This time it was an electrical storm, the worst she had seen at sea. The swells were up to 39 feet high and her boat capsized three times. Nevertheless, Jessica managed to ride out the storm with only the mainsail torn in two places, which she was able to fix.

After a whopping 210 days at sea, on May 15, 2010, three days before her 17th birthday, Jessica steered "Ella's Pink Lady" into Sydney Harbor, where over 100,000 people had gathered to greet her. Her homecoming was broadcast live on Australian television. Jessica had proved to the world and those who thought she was too young and inexperienced that anything is possible if you set your mind to it and work hard.

Jessica's story is one of courage and positive thinking. Despite the obstacles, she never gave up on her dream.

MANY PEOPLE SAID SHE COULDN'T DO IT, BUT SHE PROVED THEM WRONG.

If Jessica can sail solo around the globe at just 16, you can do anything you set your mind to. Never give up when things get tough.

YOU'LL NEVER KNOW WHAT YOU ARE CAPABLE OF UNTIL YOU TRY.

Adele

SINGER (1998 – PRESENT)

Adele is a world-famous singer and songwriter
from the United Kingdom.

÷ Be **BRAVE**
and **FEARLESS**
to know that
even if you do make
a **WRONG DECISION**,
you're **making it**
for **GOOD REASON**. ÷

– Adele

Born on May 5, 1998, Adele Laurie Blue Adkins (or Adele, as she is known throughout the world) had a challenging start in life.

Adele was born in a working-class area of London, England, called Tottenham. She was only young when her father left, leaving her mother, Penny, to raise Adele.

It wasn't long until Adele started singing. At just four years old, she became fascinated by the voices on the records her mother would play at home. Adele had natural talent, which became even more unique as the years passed.

Adele and her mother moved often during her childhood, but she always considered London her home. She wrote one of her first songs, "Hometown Glory," about an area of London, West Norwood, where she lived for only a short time. But it was during her time living in Brockwell Park that Adele truly fell in love with making music. While in Brockwell Park, she would write and perform songs on her guitar for her friends. Her experience exploring her passion for music within this encouraging community inspired her song "Million Years Ago."

Adele looked up to the example set by her mother, who taught her that if she worked hard and had a positive outlook on life, then anything was possible. But Adele ultimately had only one goal: to sing professionally. She did not enjoy school and found education challenging, but that did not stop Adele from pursuing her dream.

Adele got the opportunity of a lifetime when she auditioned to become a student at the world-famous BRIT School for Performing Arts in London. She auditioned for a place at the prestigious college by singing a song she had listened to frequently as a child. This song was Stevie Wonder's "Free." The BRIT School teachers were so impressed that Adele was accepted as a student.

Adele wasn't the only rising star in her class at the BRIT School. She graduated in 2006 with fellow superstars-in-the-making Jessie J and Leona Lewis. But even surrounded by such amazingly talented singers, Adele had to overcome a lot of self-doubts. She even considered a different career path while studying at the BRIT School and thought about giving up on her dream of becoming a singer altogether. Fortunately, her dream was stronger than her fears, and her hard work soon paid off.

After Adele graduated from the BRIT School, a friend posted some of her songs on the social media site MySpace. Never in her wildest dreams could she have imagined that she would receive a phone call from a leading music producer a few weeks later. Adele wondered at first if the call was actually a prank, but by September 2006, she was one of the budding stars of the record label XL.

In the years that followed, Adele became one of the world's most famous and influential musicians, selling over 120 million records. She has won countless awards, including 15 Grammys, while her debut album "19" has become one of the best-selling albums of all time. She has also performed with some of the most famous artists in the world. Yet Adele credits much of her success to the example set by her mother, Penny, who worked tirelessly to give her daughter the opportunities she needed to chase her dreams.

THE SKY'S THE LIMIT WHEN YOU HAVE A POSITIVE OUTLOOK AND THE DETERMINATION TO SUCCEED.

Adele's story shows that hard work combined with supportive family and friends makes the impossible seem possible. Adele never gave up on her dreams, even when things were tough.

Over to You

Wow…just wow. What courageous women.

It takes a lot of courage to pursue a dream, especially when the odds are against you. But as we've seen from the stories of Malala, Bethany, Jessica, and Adele, it's essential to never give up. The best way to achieve your dreams is to have the right mindset.

BELIEVE IN YOURSELF AND KNOW THAT YOU ARE CAPABLE OF ANYTHING.

As Jessica Watson said, "You don't have to be someone special to achieve something amazing."

Activity - Courage Collage

What does courage mean to you? On the following page, use drawings, quotes, or stories about people that represent courage to you and create a collage. Underneath each picture, write what it means to you.

For example:

- A drawing of someone speaking in front of a crowd could represent overcoming the fear of public speaking.

- A drawing of someone rock climbing could represent conquering your fears and pushing yourself outside your comfort zone.

Use the collage as a reminder...

YOU ARE CAPABLE OF ANYTHING YOU SET YOUR MIND TO!

Courage Collage

Add drawings, quotes or write about people you admire or who motivate you. They could be friends, family or famous people who have shown courage.

COURAGE IS

Standing up to bullies

My Hero

CHAPTER 2

SELF-BELIEF AND THE MINDSET OF A WINNER

If you **WANT** something, go **GET IT**. Period.

— Will Smith

Have you ever wanted something so badly but didn't think you could achieve it? Perhaps you wanted to be the lead in the school play, but you were too shy to audition. Or maybe you wanted to sing in front of an audience but were too scared to perform.

But what if it doesn't matter if you're not the best or if you don't have any experience? What if all that matters is that you try? What if all it takes is to take that first step, even if you're scared?

That's the mindset of a winner.

A WINNER IS SOMEONE WHO TRIES, EVEN WHEN THEY'RE SCARED. THEY DON'T GIVE UP, EVEN WHEN THEY FAIL.

If you have the mindset of a winner, anything is possible. Just ask these people….

Jasmin Paris

ULTRARUNNER (1983 – PRESENT)

Jasmin Paris is a record-breaking British ultrarunner and environmentalist who became the first woman to win the 268-mile Spine Race, beating her closest competitor by 15 hours. She achieved this while expressing breast milk for her young baby at aid stations along the way.

> **I STRUGGLE with having ENOUGH TIME, but NOT MOTIVATION.**
>
> – Jasmin Paris

Do you like running? Perhaps you run to school or run around the block? Maybe you are part of a sports team, or you just like going for a run by yourself? But have you ever thought about running 268 miles?

Jasmin Paris did. Not only did she think about it, she went out and did it! And what's more, she smashed the previous record by 12 hours.

Born in 1983, Jasmin Paris grew up in a small town in the Peak District of England with her parents and three brothers. Instilled in her from a young age was a belief that if you put your mind to something, you can do it. When she was 11 years old, she decided she wanted to be a veterinarian. She pursued that dream throughout school until graduating with a degree in veterinary science in 2008.

Once she was finished with school, she started her career close to home. It was here that she began running, joining a local running club and taking part in fell running, which is a type of off-road hill running.

While most long-distance runners start training in their youth, Jasmin arrived late to the sport at 25 years of age. However, she had lived an outdoor life and was used to hiking up mountains and backpacking, so the transition to running was relatively easy.

Jasmin fell in love with running almost immediately.

Fast forward a few years, including a move to Scotland, and she began to compete more seriously, winning national fell running championships in 2014 and 2015. Jasmin continued to collect more victories and set record-breaking times, not just for the women's division, but also for the men's. In 2016, she was crowned world champion at the Extreme Skyrunner World Series, an event for high-altitude endurance athletes.

A year later, Jasmin and her husband, Konrad Rawlik (also an ultrarunner), became new parents to a baby girl. Jasmin had continued to train during pregnancy. She even competed in a race a week before the birth of her daughter!

Her most iconic race, and the one that made her a household name, was the 268-mile Montane Spine Race in the winter of 2019, 14 months after the birth of her daughter.

The race is a non-stop ultra marathon along a mountainous trail in England. It is regarded as one of the world's toughest endurance races. Being held in winter, it is cold and dark, so the competitors have to fight freezing temperatures, driving rain, and icy winds. In fact, it's so tough that usually, only a third of the runners complete the course.

Jasmin underwent an intense training program that involved early starts to prepare for the harsh terrain and long distance. She would wake up at 5 am each morning for her long runs and sometimes ran 80-90 miles weekly, with hours spent running up and down hills. She did all of this while being a mom to her young baby!

As if running 268 miles wasn't tough enough, Jasmin had one other challenge that her competitors did not.

DURING THE 268-MILE RACE, SHE WOULD STOP TO EXPRESS BREAST MILK FOR HER YOUNG BABY AT AID STATIONS ALONG THE WAY.

Jasmin ran the race through the day and night, navigating the course in freezing temperatures and stopping at each aid station to pump breast milk for her daughter. Realizing she would have to shorten her breaks if she wanted to win, she ran almost non-stop, with only two hours of sleep across three days.

Jasmin crossed the finish line in a record-breaking time of 83 hours, 12 minutes, and 23 seconds, becoming the first woman to win the race. A mind-blowing 15 hours later, after finally getting some proper rest, she cheered home the second-place finisher.

JASMIN'S VICTORY SHOWED THAT WOMEN CAN OVERCOME THE TRADITIONAL EXPECTATIONS PEOPLE HAVE OF THEM.

She had outrun every man in the race as a breastfeeding mom.

Her win and her dedication to being a young mother inspired women around the world and attracted the attention of the world's media. She quickly gained a large online following and appeared in newspapers, magazines, and talk shows.

Since her historic win, Jasmin has continued to race. She also co-founded The Green Runners, a club focused on teaching runners how to reduce their carbon footprint. The club was founded in response to the growing concerns about climate change.

Jasmin's extraordinary accomplishments show us that anything is possible with hard work, determination, and a winning mindset. She came to the sport relatively late but became one of the best ultrarunners in the world. In addition, her wins brought the issues of gender equality and climate change to the center of the running community.

Like Jasmin, each of us can set out to accomplish huge goals.

It's NEVER TOO LATE to start RUNNING AFTER your DREAMS.

The Williams Sisters

PROFESSIONAL TENNIS PLAYERS (1980 & 1981 – PRESENT)

Venus and Serena Williams, often referred to as the "Williams sisters," are regarded as two of the greatest tennis players of all time, having dominated the women's game for over 20 years.

> When you *lose*, you **GET UP**, you **MAKE IT BETTER**, you **TRY AGAIN**.

— Serena Williams

If you follow tennis, you've probably heard of the Williams sisters.

For OVER 20 YEARS, THEY'VE DOMINATED THE WOMEN'S GAME, WINNING 30 GRAND SLAM SINGLES TITLES BETWEEN THEM.

But their rise to the top did not come without its own challenges. Starting from humble beginnings, the Williams family proved that anything is possible with dedication and hard work.

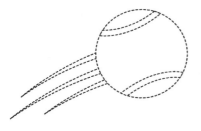

Venus, the older of the two, was born June 17, 1980, in Lynwood, California. Serena was born a year later, on September 26, 1981, in Saginaw, Michigan, to Richard Williams and Oracene Price. While the girls were still toddlers, their dad moved the family to Compton, California.

Growing up in Compton was tough. The city was known for its high crime rate, and the family of seven shared a small, two-bed home.

Richard first took Venus to the local tennis court at the tender age of four and a half, where she picked up a tennis racket and started training for the first time. Her sister, Serena, followed Venus onto the tennis court a year later.

The girl's father had no formal tennis training. He was a self-taught tennis coach, but he had confidence in his coaching skills and was determined that his girls would succeed and one day dominate the world of tennis. Their mom supported the family and believed the girls could achieve anything they set their minds to.

For the next seven years, Venus and Serena trained on the public tennis courts in the area, putting in hours of practice every day under the guidance of their parents.

Come RAIN OR SHINE, THE GIRLS WOULD PRACTICE, SOMETIMES HITTING 500 VOLLEYS BEFORE CALLING IT A DAY.

This determination to succeed, combined with years of hard work and dedication, eventually led to the girls' incredible success.

In 1991, the girls' father moved the family to Florida. He enrolled them in a professional tennis academy, where the girls trained six hours a day, six days a week, for the next four years.

Three years later, a couple of months after her 14th birthday, Venus Williams made her professional debut, winning her first-ever match as a pro. A year later, in 1995, her younger sister Serena also turned professional at 14.

Within three years, Venus had broken into the top 100 best female players and reached her first Grand Slam final. She was also named WTA Newcomer of the Year. Serena won her first

Grand Slam title in 1999 at the age of 17, becoming only the second African American woman to win a Grand Slam singles title.

The world of women's tennis had never seen anything like the two sisters. They were athletic and powerful and had a unique style of play unmatched by any other player on tour.

But this was just the beginning for Venus and Serena. They continued to climb the tennis rankings over the next couple of years and won more titles while still in their teens.

Over the next two decades, they dominated the women's game like no other players before them. They became the most successful sister act in tennis history, with a rivalry on the court helping to fuel their success.

The sisters won 30 Grand Slam singles titles, 14 Grand Slam doubles championships and four Olympic gold medals. They were also ranked No. 1 in the world numerous times for both singles and doubles. Serena held the joint record for the most consecutive weeks at the top spot with 186.

AFTER THE FRENCH OPEN IN 2002, THEY BECAME THE FIRST SISTERS TO BE RANKED NO. 1 AND 2 IN THE WORLD AT THE SAME TIME.

The Williams sisters have not only rewritten the history books, they have also inspired a new generation of female tennis players. They are living proof that anything is possible if you have the talent, determination, and work ethic to succeed.

IF VENUS AND SERENA CAN DO IT, SO CAN YOU.

With the right mindset, you have the power to achieve anything you set your mind to. Think like a winner and never lose sight of the end goal, no matter what it takes.

McKenzie Coan

SWIMMER (1996 – PRESENT)

McKenzie Coan is a record-breaking American Paralympic swimmer who has overcome numerous obstacles to achieve her dreams in the pool.

I BREAK,
but I
GET BACK UP
again, and I
KEEP GOING.

- McKenzie Coan

Have you ever broken a bone? McKenzie Coan has. In fact, she has suffered almost 100 fractures in her lifetime. But that hasn't stopped her from becoming one of the top Paralympic swimmers in the world.

Born on June 14, 1996, in Georgia, McKenzie was just 19 days old when doctors diagnosed her with osteogenesis imperfecta, or brittle bone disease. Brittle bone disease is a disorder that results in bones breaking easily.

After her diagnosis, the doctors told McKenzie's parents that she would probably never be able to walk, sit up straight, or live a long life. McKenzie's parents refused to accept this prognosis and encouraged their daughter to live an active, everyday life. McKenzie would soon prove the doctors wrong.

At four years old, McKenzie was already developing a love for swimming from her time in aqua therapy sessions, where she could leave her wheelchair behind. After her brothers joined the swim team, she was determined to follow the same path. At age five, she swam on her own for the first time to qualify for the swim team and begin her journey to the Paralympic Games.

The Paralympics are a sporting event for athletes with disabilities. They are the world's second-largest multi-sport event after the Olympic Games.

At eight years old, McKenzie had her first taste of the Paralympics when she was recruited into a Paralympic sports program and started training with and competing against other para-athletes.

She spent the next few years fully committed to qualifying for the Paralympic Games, despite enduring many broken bones throughout her training. Although she just missed out on qualification for the 2008 Beijing Paralympics, McKenzie was determined to join the team for the 2012 Games in London.

 Her hard work and determination paid off. At age 16, McKenzie made the US team and traveled to London for the Paralympics. She made the finals and swam to sixth place in the 400m freestyle. However, she promised to return to the next Games and earn a spot on the podium.

Sure enough, McKenzie returned fitter and stronger four years later for the 2016 Rio de Janeiro Paralympic Games, where she swam to three gold medals, winning the 50m, 100m, and 400m freestyle events. She also earned a silver in the relay.

Her prolific wins, coupled with her infectious smile, shot McKenzie to worldwide fame. And yet she is far more than just a champion swimmer.

MCKENZIE IS ALSO A FIERCE ADVOCATE FOR THE DISABLED COMMUNITY, SPEAKING OUT ABOUT HOW HER DISABILITY WAS NEVER A WEAKNESS BUT RATHER HER STRENGTH.

Since the 2016 Games, McKenzie has continued swimming, breaking many of her own records. She even trained in a homemade pool in her garage during the pandemic to prepare for the 2020 Tokyo Paralympics.

In 2021, she released an autobiography about her incredible journey. She's also studying law at the University of Baltimore. She continues to help make the world more accessible for disabled female athletes like herself.

McKenzie has accomplished a lot for someone who is still young. She is an excellent example of what is possible if you have self-belief and a positive mindset. She could have easily given up after breaking her bones many times, but she didn't.

NEVER GIVE UP ON YOUR DREAMS, NO MATTER HOW OFTEN YOU FAIL OR HOW HARD THINGS GET.

Cynthia Marshall

Business Executive (1959 – Present)

Cynthia Marshall is a business executive who overcame adversity to become the first African American female appointed head of a National Basketball Association team in the US.

CRY like a baby, FIGHT like a girl, and CHANGE the world like a woman.

- Cynthia Marshall

You might have heard the saying: "When life gives you lemons, make lemonade." When Cynthia Marshall faced some of life's biggest challenges, she didn't just make lemonade — she broke down barriers and changed the world. As the current head of the Dallas Mavericks, she is the first African American female CEO in the National Basketball Association.

Cynthia was born in 1959 in Birmingham, Alabama. Still, she spent much of her life growing up in the Eastern Hills housing project in Richmond, California. At the time, the housing project was known for being one of the more dangerous places to live in the city, plagued with gangs and violence.

Financially, things were tough, and crime was never too far away. But Cynthia's mom set goals and provided structure and routine, believing that education was the path out of the projects. Cynthia thrived on this routine. She felt safe and welcome at school and found that it was a place where she could excel. With her positive, can-do attitude, she would not allow her circumstances to derail her.

When Cynthia was 15 years old, her mom, Carolyn, secretly filed for divorce from her sometimes violent dad and fled with her kids. The family spent that summer picking up the pieces of their lives, with education becoming a refuge for Cynthia. More determined than ever to rise above her circumstances and make something of her life, she stayed focused on what she wanted to accomplish.

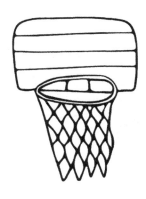

This determination and resourcefulness paid off when, in 1977, Cynthia became the first African American girl to be elected president of her graduating class. It was a historic moment for her, but it would not be the last time she was to make history.

After receiving offers for five full scholarships, she chose to head to the University of California, Berkeley, where she became the first African American cheerleader. She also acquired the nickname "Cynt," short for "Cynt the sprint," from her fellow track team members — a name she still goes by today.

After college, Cynt joined AT&T, a large telecom company. Soon after that, she married her college sweetheart, Kenneth Marshall. After struggling to have kids, Cynt gave birth to a premature daughter, who sadly passed away six months later. Heartbroken, Cynt picked up the pieces of her life. She and Kenneth went on to adopt four children from the foster care system.

Slowly but surely, Cynt climbed the corporate ladder. She was appointed president of AT&T North Carolina in 2007. She became the first African American to chair the state's chamber of commerce.

During her time in North Carolina, Cynt was diagnosed with cancer. She resolved to fight the disease and be there for her family. After five long years and treatments that taxed her health, she was finally declared cancer-free.

Cynt continued her tireless efforts to transform AT&T into a diverse and inclusive workplace, but after 36 years, she decided to leave the company in 2017 to set up her own consulting firm.

A year later, she received a call from billionaire Mark Cuban, the owner of the Dallas Mavericks, a professional basketball team that plays in the National Basketball Association (NBA). He was on the hunt for a strong leader to turn the company around, and the name that kept popping up was Cynt Marshall.

Cynt and Mark struck a deal, and in February 2018 Cynt became the first African American woman to lead an NBA basketball team. Today, she continues to blaze the trail, inspiring women through her role as CEO of the Mavericks.

Cynthia's story is not only about the determination to succeed against the odds. It's also about getting up when life knocks you down and never giving up.

WITH THE RIGHT MINDSET AND SELF-BELIEF, YOU, TOO, CAN FACE THE CHALLENGES THAT LIFE THROWS AT YOU AND COME OUT VICTORIOUS.

Over to You

Jasmin Paris, The Williams sisters, McKenzie Coan, and Cynthia Marshall are all very different women who have achieved success in different ways. Still, there are some key things that they all have in common.

ONE OF THEM IS SELF-BELIEF.

All five of these inspiring women have overcome considerable challenges in their lives, and one of the things that helped them to do so was self-belief.

THEY ALL BELIEVED IN THEMSELVES, EVEN WHEN OTHER PEOPLE DOUBTED THEM.

They knew they could achieve their goals, no matter how difficult they might seem.

What exactly is self-belief?

Self-belief is when you have confidence in your own ability to achieve something. It's knowing you can do something, even if other people don't think you can.

Self-belief is vital because it motivates you to keep going, even when things are tough. It helps you get back up after you've been knocked down.

Another attribute these women have is a winner's mindset.

They APPROACH EVERYTHING with a POSITIVE ATTITUDE and the BELIEF that THEY CAN SUCCEED.

They don't let setbacks stop them from achieving their goals.

If you want TO BE SUCCESSFUL in anything, you must BELIEVE IN YOURSELF, BE POSITIVE, and always LOOK FOR OPPORTUNITIES.

Activity - The Power of Yet

Have you heard of the story about the young girl trying to learn to do something new? Whenever she tried and failed, instead of giving up, she said,

"I can't do it...YET."

This is a great way to approach failure.

Just because you can't do something YET, doesn't mean you never will be able to do it.

KEEP TRYING, AND DON'T GIVE UP.

Next time you feel down because you can't do something, remember: You simply can't do it YET. With a bit of practice, you will be able to do it!

Write down some of the things you want to learn how to do but feel like you can't yet, then commit to practicing one of those things every day until you feel confident you can do it.

For example:

- I want to learn how to play the guitar, but I can't yet.

- I want to learn how to speak French, but I can't yet.

- I want to learn how to code, but I can't yet.

Don't let the fact that you can't do something YET stop you from trying. With a bit of practice, anything is possible!

The Power of YET

I am not good at singing

YET

YET

YET

YET

YET

CHAPTER 3

NEVER GIVING UP & BEATING THE ODDS

WHERE there is

no **STRUGGLE,**

there is

no **STRENGTH.**

– Oprah Winfrey

Have you heard the saying: "If at first you don't succeed, try, try again?" This is called perseverance, which means to "keep going even when it's difficult."

It's like when you're LEARNING to RIDE A BIKE.

At first, finding your balance is challenging, and you might fall off a few times.

But IF you PERSEVERE and KEEP TRYING, EVENTUALLY, you START TO GET THE HANG OF IT. Before you know it, you're RIDING AROUND LIKE A PRO!

The same is true for anything in life. To achieve something, you must persevere, even when it's tough. You need to be determined to keep going until you reach your goal.

In this chapter, we will explore the stories of four successful women who have overcome enormous challenges to achieve their goals. They all have one key thing in common: They never gave up.

Even when the going got tough and they faced setbacks, they persevered and eventually achieved their goals.

Let's get started....

Claudette Colvin

CIVIL RIGHTS ACTIVIST (1939 – PRESENT)

Claudette Colvin is an American pioneer of the 1950s civil rights movement.

> ⟫ **When it comes to**
>
> # JUSTICE,
>
> **there is no easy way**
>
> # TO GET IT.
>
> **You have to**
>
> # TAKE A STAND.... ⟫

— Claudette Colvin

Imagine this: It's 1955, and you're a 15-year-old student in Montgomery, Alabama. You're on your way home from school when the bus driver tells you to give up your seat to a white passenger.

You refuse because you know it's unjust. The bus driver becomes angry and calls the police, and you are arrested and taken to the police station.

This is precisely what happened to Claudette Colvin.

Born on September 5, 1939, in Montgomery, Alabama, Claudette was no stranger to the effects of poverty growing up. Life was a daily struggle for her dad, C.P. Austin, and her mom, Mary Jane Gadson, as they scraped together enough money each day to provide for Claudette and her six sisters.

When her dad walked out on the family, and her mom could not financially support them, Claudette and her sister Delphine moved to a little country town called Pine Level to live with their great aunt Mary Anne and her husband, Q.P Colvin. The couple provided the two girls with stability and a loving family home and eventually adopted them.

Claudette was now a Colvin.

Life was simple in Pine Level, with its schoolhouse, general store, and church. But all of that was about to change for Claudette when her adopted mom inherited a house in King Hill, Montgomery, when Claudette was eight. The family's new home — a small frame house in a tiny hilltop development — was sandwiched between two white neighborhoods.

Despite missing her life in Pine Level, Claudette soon adjusted to city life. But Claudette eventually began to realize how the rules of racial segregation (the separation of white and black people) dictated her life in Montgomery. For example, she could shop in white stores, but they wouldn't let her try anything on. She could walk through nearby Oak Park, but if she tried to sit down on one of the benches, the police would arrest her. The laws that kept white people and African Americans from learning together, playing together, working together, and riding buses and trains together made Claudette angry.

In 1952, on Claudette's 13th birthday, two weeks before she was due to begin her first year at high school, Delphine died of polio. After that, Claudette was determined to put her mind to her studies and focus. She was an A student, intelligent and well-mannered. But Claudette thought differently than a lot of kids at her school. She wanted to go to college, and she wanted the kind of education provided at schools for white pupils.

This was a turning point in her life. She started thinking about racism and prejudice, which motivated her to join the National Association for the Advancement of Colored People (NAACP) Youth Council. It was here that she formed a close relationship with her mentor, Rosa Parks, known today as the mother of the civil rights movement in America. Little by little, Claudette began to develop a mission for herself. She would become a lawyer and fight against the injustices forced on her fellow African Americans.

On March 2, 1955, when Claudette was 15 years old, she set in motion a chain of events that forever changed the course of American history. That Wednesday afternoon, she and a few friends boarded the bus that would take them home from school. As usual, she paid for her ticket, walked halfway down the aisle, and took a seat in the middle section of the bus.

Under the system of racial segregation, African Americans were required to sit in the back half of the bus, whereas white people sat at the front. The middle section, where Claudette sat, was considered unreserved. But if all the seats at the front of the bus were full, the African Americans in the central area had to give up their seats to the white passengers.

As the bus followed its route, the front seats steadily filled up with white passengers who had finished work for the day.

As more white people boarded the bus, Claudette noticed a white woman standing in the aisle between the four seats in her row. The bus driver called out that he needed the seats. As her school friends in the row got up and moved back, Claudette remained seated. She had paid for her ticket like everybody else, and there were now three empty seats in her row.

THERE AND THEN, SHE DECIDED TO TAKE A STAND.

The white woman stood, waiting for Claudette to move to the seats behind. The standoff continued until two Montgomery city police officers boarded the bus at one of the stops and arrested Claudette.

 Claudette was taken to the police station, where she was charged. Her arrest made her the center of attention wherever she went as news of what she had done spread. Unfortunately for Claudette, at her trial a couple of days later, she was found guilty of breaking the segregation law and disturbing the peace. But Claudette had set the wheels of change in motion. Later that year, she was one of five people who testified in front of a judge who ruled that bus segregation was unconstitutional. By 1956, the Supreme Court had agreed with the ruling to end bus segregation.

Claudette played a small part in changing American history. She was a young girl who took a stand against discrimination and fought for what she knew was right, even though it wasn't easy. Her actions that day sparked a flame that contributed to the civil rights movement's impact on public transportation in the US.

Just like Claudette, who believed enough to take action, you can also change the world.

NEVER GIVE UP, DESPITE YOUR STRUGGLES –
STAND TRUE TO WHAT YOU BELIEVE IN.

Nancy Wake

JOURNALIST AND SPY (1912 – 2011)

Nancy Wake was a prominent figure in the French resistance who worked as a spy for the British and saved hundreds of lives in World War II.

÷I was NEVER AFRAID. I was TOO BUSY TO BE AFRAID.÷

- Nancy Wake

Some do generations worth of work in one lifetime. Nancy Wake was one of those people.

Born in New Zealand in 1912, Nancy moved to Australia with her family when she was two.

Desperate to see the world, Nancy would often sit by the harbor and dream of running away to Paris. She was inspired by her mom's eldest sister, Aunt Hinamoa, who had run off with a whaling captain. At age 16, Nancy did just that. She ran away from home and moved to a small country town outside Sydney, where she took a nursing job.

Then, in a twist of fate that would change Nancy's life forever, Aunt Hinamoa, who had heard that Nancy had run away, sent her 300 dollars in financial assistance. In those days, this was a lot of money, enabling Nancy to fulfill her ambition and travel to Europe. So, in 1932, she waved goodbye to Sydney and set sail for London.

When she arrived in London, her money was fast running out. Using what was left, Nancy enrolled in a journalism course, which she hoped might help her secure some work. The gamble paid off, and she was offered a post in Paris by an American newspaper.

But Europe was changing fast. Hitler was rising to power, and the Nazis were taking over Germany. In 1933, soon after she arrived in France, Nancy visited Vienna and Berlin. There, she saw the terrible treatment the Jews were receiving at the hands of the Nazis. This affected Nancy deeply, and she made a vow to do everything she could to make life difficult for Hitler and his forces.

In 1939, she met and married wealthy French industrialist Henri Fiocca. The following year, in May 1940, Hitler's forces crossed the border and invaded France. Nancy was not content to stay home while her husband was called up to fight for the French army, so she suggested using one of the vans from his factory and turning it into an ambulance. And so it was that she joined a small, voluntary ambulance unit that transported refugees from the north to the south of France. The work was dangerous, challenging, and upsetting, and her ambulance was often bombarded by gunfire.

One evening, while waiting for her husband at a hotel in Paris, a chance meeting with a French soldier threw Nancy into the secret world of the French resistance (an unofficial army formed by French citizens to fight the Germans). As Madame Fiocca, the glamorous wife of a Marseilles businessman, Nancy was unlikely to be stopped and searched, so she could carry essential information across the country. Nancy joined the resistance and was soon ferrying radio transmitters and information to other towns.

She eventually met Captain Ian Garrow, who asked her to help captured Allied soldiers (from Great Britain, the United States, and the Soviet Union) escape from France to neutral Spain.

Very quickly, Nancy became a crucial link in the escape line. But by now, the Nazi German secret police (the Gestapo) were looking for a woman fitting Nancy's description. Referred to as "The White Mouse" because she was so hard to catch, she now had a bounty of five million Francs on her head and was the Gestapo's most wanted person.

Nancy was on the run. She was a wanted woman, forced to flee from safehouse to safehouse in her attempts to elude the Gestapo. In 1943, realizing she was running out of time and that her capture would mean certain death, she fled France for England, leaving her husband behind. It was a difficult journey over the Pyrenees Mountains, first to Spain and then to England, where she eventually made it to London. While waiting for Henri to join her, Nancy was approached by the Special Operations Executive and asked to become a secret agent for them. Nancy was delighted. This was precisely the type of work she wanted to do in the war effort, despite being told that she stood a 50-50 chance of surviving her life as a spy.

On April 29, 1944, after a period of training, Nancy parachuted into Nazi-occupied France under the codename "Hélène." Her job was to act as a link between the local French resistance fighters  and London and help organize weapons and supplies for the group before D-Day (The Allied invasion of Normandy). But tragic news awaited Nancy when France was finally liberated from Nazi occupation. Her husband had been killed by the Gestapo the year before.

Nancy returned to London, receiving medals for her bravery and work in the war. She lived out her remaining years traveling between Australia and England.

Nancy Wake was a force of nature with a fighting spirit to match. She never wavered from the vow she had made to herself to make life difficult for Hitler and his forces, despite all the obstacles she had to face.

Nancy NEVER GAVE IN and NEVER GAVE UP.

Remember, it always seems impossible until you do it. No matter who you are, you can accomplish anything you want with the right mindset. The path you take may have obstacles as you strive toward your dream, but it's the lessons you learn from overcoming these obstacles that matter.

Be BOLD, be COURAGEOUS, and NEVER GIVE UP.

Greta Thunberg

ENVIRONMENTALIST (2003 – PRESENT)

Greta Thunberg is a world-famous Swedish environmental activist and campaigner.

> ⁓ *You are* NEVER
>
> *TOO SMALL*
>
> *to make a*
>
> DIFFERENCE. ⁓
>
> - Greta Thunberg

Some people are born with a mission. They know what they want to do from a very young age. Greta Thunberg is one of those people.

Born on January 3, 2003, Greta grew up in Sweden, in the capital city of Stockholm. Greta was a quiet and attentive child. When she was just eight years old, she found out about the existence of something called "climate change."

Climate change is an important environmental issue that looks at how human beings have contributed to the long-term changes in temperature and typical weather patterns around the world.

Greta was deeply affected by what she learned about climate change and its potential impact. She began to despair when she realized how urgently people needed to act to stop it and how little people were doing to help reverse its effects. When she was 11 years old, she stopped talking and eating and struggled with depression.

She was later diagnosed with Asperger's syndrome, obsessive-compulsive disorder (OCD), and a condition where she found it hard to speak, called selective mutism. This was a lot for Greta to overcome at a young age, but it didn't stop her from dreaming of a better world. She finally decided to act.

Greta was young and still studying at school when she decided to be an environmental activist. Her parents were not so encouraging of Greta's dream at first. Being an environmental activist was a full-time job for someone as committed as Greta. She would sometimes miss school to  attend important rallies — something her father wasn't keen on. But her parents also saw how happy activism made her and eventually encouraged their daughter.

Greta's activism encouraged her parents to change their daily routines and habits. She insisted on living in a vegan household, which meant no more meat, fish, eggs, or dairy products. She also encouraged her parents to start "upcycling," which meant that everyday items that would otherwise have been thrown away were reused and given a new purpose. But the most significant change happened when Greta asked her parents to avoid flying whenever possible.

Flying on planes is a significant contributor to climate change, increasing a person's "carbon footprint." A carbon footprint is the total amount of greenhouse gasses an individual or family produces. Reducing your carbon footprint is one of the best things you can do to help fight climate change. Making small, everyday decisions like cycling instead of driving, eating less meat, or reducing flights can make a big difference.

 Greta's mother was a successful opera singer who flew worldwide for work, but Greta convinced her that there were other ways to travel, like taking the train, which has a much smaller carbon footprint than flying. It was a big change for the family, but they were willing to make it because they supported and believed in Greta's cause.

In 2018, when Greta was just 15, she began the activism work that would eventually make her a household name. After Sweden suffered one of its hottest summers, Greta decided enough was enough. She chose to strike. On August 20, 2018, Greta Thunberg skipped school to protest in front of the Swedish Parliament. She held a hand-painted sign that said:

"SCHOOL STRIKE FOR CLIMATE."

Greta continued to protest every Friday and used her Instagram account to document her strike action, gaining her global attention. She was soon joined by other students and received support from other environmental activists. The Fridays for Future movement had begun.

The Fridays for Future movement is a worldwide protest against climate change where students are encouraged to hold demonstrations. The goal is to pressure political leaders into taking action on climate change.

Greta's message was simple:

IF YOU DON'T TAKE CARE OF THE PLANET, THERE WON'T BE A FUTURE FOR ANYONE, INCLUDING TODAY'S YOUNG PEOPLE.

In the months following the strike, Greta was invited to speak at climate change rallies across Europe. Her speech at the 2018 United Nations Climate Change Conference became a viral sensation on social media. Greta worked tirelessly to attend as many rallies as possible to promote her message of change, even crossing the Atlantic in a sailboat to minimize her carbon footprint.

IN 2019, GRETA WAS NOMINATED FOR A NOBEL PEACE PRIZE AND WAS THE YOUNGEST PERSON TO BE NAMED TIME MAGAZINE'S PERSON OF THE YEAR.

Greta Thunberg has since become one of the world's leading voices on climate change and has inspired millions worldwide to take action. She is considered by many people to be one of the most influential young people on the planet. She has won countless awards for her work and is proof that anyone can overcome  the odds if they believe in themselves and never give up on chasing their dreams.

Wilma Glodean Rudolph

ATHLETE (1940 – 1994)

Wilma Rudolph overcame many obstacles to become the first American female athlete to win three gold medals in track and field at a single Olympics.

> ❖ **I BELIEVE**
> *in* **ME**
> **more** *than anything*
> *in this* **world**. ❖
>
> — **Wilma Rudolph**

If determination were a person, her name would be Wilma Rudolph!

Wilma was born in 1940 in the small farming town of Saint Bethlehem, Tennessee. She was one of 22 in the family, and because she was born prematurely, she was so small and frail that her parents feared she would not survive. But Wilma was a fighter.

Shortly after her birth, the family moved to nearby Clarksville, where she was left in the care of her four elder siblings while her parents were at work. From birth, it was a struggle for survival for Wilma. By age four, she had already suffered scarlet fever and double pneumonia. When she was five, she contracted polio. She survived but lost the use of her left leg. Doctors told her she would never walk again, but Wilma's parents were not about to give up. Instead, using what little money they had, they devoted their time to helping their daughter.

Once a week, Wilma and her mom boarded a bus and traveled 90 miles to a clinic, where she received treatment. While at home, her older siblings took turns massaging and exercising her leg so that, by the time she was eight, she was walking with a leg brace by the time she was eight. Not long after, Wilma was fitted with a special shoe that enabled her to get around and go to school. She constantly pushed herself by playing basketball with her brothers in the backyard, never allowing her disability to hold her back.

Finally, one day, when she was 11, Wilma tossed aside her special shoe to prove she could walk like anyone else. But that was just the beginning for Wilma Rudolph. Not content to sit on the sidelines, she was determined to participate in sports and compensate for the lost time.

She became an all-state basketball champion, breaking the girl's state record. Her success on the basketball court attracted the attention of the track coach at Tennessee State University. He saw the potential in her to become a great runner. In 1956, at just 16 years of age, she qualified for and competed in the Olympic games in Melbourne, Australia, where she won a bronze medal in the 4x100 relay.

Wilma was not content to stop there. In fact, her first taste of Olympic success made her more determined than ever to succeed. Four years later, at the 1960 summer Olympics in Rome, she made history by becoming the first American woman to win three gold medals in track and field at a single Olympics. This performance earned her the title "the fastest woman in the world."

And it didn't end there! Wilma broke down gender barriers by becoming the first woman to compete in the New York Athletic Club meet, the Penn relays, and the Los Angeles Times Games. Her fame was opening doors that had long been closed to female athletes, who were still considered second class, no matter their achievements.

It was not just on the track that Wilma's presence was felt. Upon her return to her hometown of Clarksville after her Olympic triumph, she declined to attend her homecoming parade unless people of all races could attend.

After winning the Associated Press Female Athlete of the Year award in 1961, Wilma took to the track one last time in 1962. Although she won the 100-meter and the relay, at 22 years of age, she knew it was time for her to retire. Taking off her track shoes for the last time, she signed them and gave them to a little boy. Wilma returned to college, graduated with a BA in education, and became a second-grade teacher and high school track coach.

Over the next two decades, Wilma continued to be a major presence in amateur sports, working with Olympic committees and setting up the Wilma Rudolf Foundation to encourage young, disadvantaged children to participate in athletics.

Tragically, Wilma's life was cut short in November 1994, at the age of 54, when she died at her home in Nashville, Tennessee. "The Tornado," as she was affectionately called, had forever changed the world of athletics for women. Her hard work, determination, and, most importantly, the fact that she never gave up, even though the odds were stacked against her, testify to what sheer willpower and perseverance can achieve.

Just like Wilma, you, too, can overcome the obstacles you find along your path in life. The challenge is to chip away at them and never give up until they no longer stand in your way.

ANYTHING IS POSSIBLE WITH SHEER DETERMINATION. JUST SET A GOAL AND GO FOR IT, NO MATTER HOW FAR-FETCHED IT MAY SEEM TO OTHERS.

Over to You

Do you ever have a feeling that you want to quit? Perhaps it's practicing a musical instrument or doing homework when you'd prefer to be playing outside. It can be tough to keep going when you don't feel like it.

You're not alone. Everyone feels like this at times. But as we have seen in this chapter, the people who achieve great things usually don't give up when things get tough. They keep going.

Claudette Colvin took a stand against racial segregation when she was just 15.

Nancy Wake was a World War II hero who fought against the Nazis.

Greta Thunberg became a world-famous environmental activist.

Wilma Rudolph overcame polio and became one of the greatest athletes in history.

These women have one thing in common: They never gave up.

If you're feeling like giving up, remember the people in this chapter and think about how they persevered through tough times.

YOU CAN DO IT TOO!

Activity - Things You Won't Ever Give Up

What is important to you? What are you passionate about?

What are some things you would never give up on, no matter how hard things got?

These things can be big or small. They can be anything that you feel strongly about.

FOR EXAMPLE, SOME MIGHT SAY THEY WOULD NEVER GIVE UP ON THEIR DREAMS, NO MATTER HOW IMPOSSIBLE THEY SEEM. OTHERS MIGHT SAY THEY WOULD NEVER GIVE UP ON THEIR FAMILY OR FRIENDS, EVEN WHEN THINGS ARE TOUGH.

Think about the things that are important to you and write them down.

These things can be your guide in life, helping you to stay focused on what's truly important.

THINGS YOU WON'T ever give up...

I will never give up...

CHAPTER 4

TAKING RISKS
& OVERCOMING
FAILURE

Just because you

 fail once

DOESN'T MEAN

you're gonna fail

AT EVERYTHING.

- Marilyn Monroe

TAKING RISKS IS SCARY!

That's because you know you might fail, which can be tough, especially if you've tried your hardest.

BUT FAILURE IS A PART OF LIFE.

Everyone experiences it at some point.

AND YOU ARE GOING TO FAIL.

Sorry, but it's true — and that's OK!

FAILURE IS AN ESSENTIAL PART OF SUCCESS.

Think of failure as a stepping-stone to success.

EACH TIME YOU FAIL, YOU LEARN SOMETHING NEW.

Without failure, you would never learn and grow. You would never know what you're capable of.

In this chapter, we'll meet four inspirational women who have taken risks and, at some point, failed. In fact, they've all experienced some pretty big failures. But they didn't let that stop them. They picked themselves up and tried again.

J.K. Rowling

AUTHOR (1965 – PRESENT)

J.K. Rowling is the creator of the "Harry Potter" fantasy series and a bestselling author, screenwriter, and philanthropist.

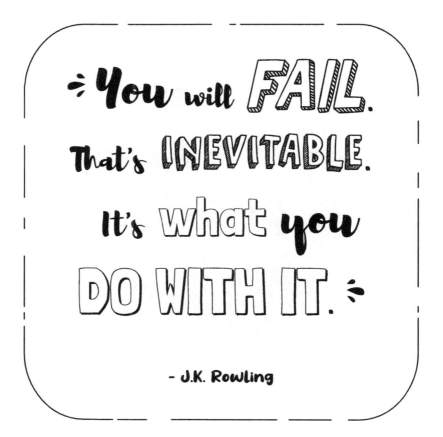

You will **FAIL**. That's **INEVITABLE**. It's **what you DO WITH IT**.

- J.K. Rowling

Imagine spending the best part of your life writing a book, only to be rejected by 12 different publishers. This happened to J.K. Rowling when she was trying to get her first book, "Harry Potter and the Philosopher's Stone," published.

Thankfully, she didn't give up and finally found a publisher willing to take a chance on her book. The rest, as they say, is history.

Born on July 31, 1965, in Yate, England, Jo was a quiet child growing up with her parents and younger sister. Drawn to storytelling and books from an early age, she was always a voracious reader with a vivid imagination.

Inspired by her parent's love of reading, she often invented stories to entertain her younger sister. When she was just six years old, her family moved to the village of Tutshill, which she would later use as the model for the fictional town of Godric's Hollow in her "Harry Potter" series.

At her new school in Tutshill, shy Jo found refuge in her English classes. Passionate about reading and writing, she wrote her first short story at age 11 about seven cursed diamonds and the people who owned them.

When Jo was 15, her mom Anne was diagnosed with multiple sclerosis, a progressive central nervous system disease. Home

life was difficult, but she continued to excel at school and was appointed head girl in her final year at high school. After school, Jo had to make a major decision. Although she wanted to be a writer, her parents encouraged her to study for a degree to have a "backup" career. After being rejected by Oxford University and following her parents' wishes, Jo went to learn French and classics at the University of Exeter.

After graduating, she moved to London, working as a researcher and secretary, among other jobs. She also continued to write in her spare time. But everything changed when her boyfriend from college asked her to move to Manchester with him. While delayed on a train from Manchester to London, the idea of Harry Potter and many of the main characters came to her. Looking out the window, she had a vision of a young boy with black hair and glasses and knew he was a wizard. Jo spent the rest of that train ride mulling over Harry and his story.

From that day on, Harry Potter was foremost in Jo's thoughts. She dropped all her other writing projects and started laying out the plot for her book. But the next few years were tough for Jo. First, her mom died after her long battle with multiple sclerosis. Then, her apartment was robbed a short time later. Jo took this as a sign that it was time to change her life.

In 1991, at age 26, Jo moved to Portugal to teach English. There, she met and married Jorge Arantes. They had a daughter, Jessica, a year later. But her marriage soon broke down, leaving Jo to support herself and her daughter. She moved back to the UK, this time to Edinburgh, Scotland, to live with her sister.

While staying with her sister, Jo eventually plucked up the courage and told her about Harry Potter. Dianne loved it. With her encouragement, Jo resolved to finish the first Harry Potter book and make it public.

With no money and a daughter to support, life was hard. She had to rely on government benefits to help support her and her daughter while working when she could. But she was determined to finish her novel, writing in cafes, where it was warm and more comfortable.

Finally, in 1995, she was done. She sent a copy of the first three chapters of her manuscript to an agent and a publisher but received rejection letters from them two weeks later. Fortunately, Jo was determined. It had taken her five years to write her novel, and she wasn't giving up now. She sent the manuscript to another agent, Christopher Little, who agreed to represent her.

THE BOOK WAS SENT OUT TO 12 PUBLISHERS, ALL OF WHOM REJECTED IT.

This would prove a lucky number for Jo, as the 13th publisher she sent it to, Bloomsbury, accepted it. Fearing the book would not appeal to young boys if they knew it was written by a female, the publishers asked Jo to provide another initial to her name. She chose "K" for Kathleen, her grandmother's name.

In June 1997, Bloomsbury published the first Harry Potter book, printing an initial run of just 500 books. Meanwhile, Jo received a grant and a small fee that would enable her to continue writing while supporting her daughter.

Jo went on to write six more titles in the Harry Potter series, each a record-breaking success.

The HARRY POTTER SERIES HAS SOLD OVER 500 MILLION COPIES AND IS

THE BESTSELLING SERIES OF ALL TIME.

The books have been translated into 70 different languages, and between 2001 and 2011, they were adapted into a hugely successful film series.

Jo's passion for writing has not diminished, as she has published international bestselling crime and adult novels. She also supports several charities, including those that help children in need.

Jo Rowling's life is an excellent example of someone rising above self-doubt and persevering. Despite numerous rejections of her writing and the personal obstacles she had to face, she proved that anything is possible with determination and hard work.

DON'T LET THE FEAR OF FAILURE AND SELF-DOUBT HOLD YOU BACK FROM ACHIEVING WHAT YOU WANT.

Instead, believe in yourself and stand up for your dreams and ambitions. Nothing is impossible if you put your mind to it.

Mary Hardway Walker

FORMERLY ENSLAVED AMERICAN (1848 – 1969)

Mary Hardway Walker was a formerly enslaved American who became the oldest person to learn to read at age 116.

You are
never too old
to learn
SOMETHING NEW
or too young
to learn
TOO MUCH.

- Suzy Kassem

Mary Hardway Walker lived when it was tough for African American women to receive an education. Still, she didn't let discrimination get in the way of her dreams.

Mary was born into slavery in 1848, which meant she was legally owned by another person and wasn't allowed to learn to read or write. She spent most of her childhood working with her enslaved parents in Union Springs, Alabama.

At age 15, Mary was officially freed after Abraham Lincoln delivered the Emancipation Proclamation in 1863. This granted freedom to all enslaved people in the United States of America. However, this didn't stop the prejudice against African Americans, which made it difficult for Mary and other black students to get an education.

For these reasons, Mary never had a formal education. She couldn't read, write, or do math. But this did not stop her from leading a full life. After  her freedom from slavery, she quickly settled into her new life, working as a cook, cleaner, babysitter, and sandwich seller. By the time she was 20, she had a husband and one child.

She dedicated her life to motherhood for the next few decades, raising three sons with her husband in Chattanooga, Tennessee.

Mary saw considerable changes in her life. She lived through the Civil War, World War I, and World War II.

She was BORN BEFORE the RADIO was invented and ALIVE WHEN the first TELEVISION SHOW was BROADCAST.

Amazingly, by the time Mary was 114, she had outlived her husband, all her siblings, and her three sons. Sadly, she had no surviving relatives. But she stayed involved with her community, cooking meals for the neighborhood and bringing donations to the church.

In her final years, she became determined to get an education. At the age of 116, she enrolled as a student at Chattanooga Area Literacy Movement, a school taught by volunteer teach-

ers. For over a year, Mary attended one-hour classes twice a week to learn basic literacy and math.

Mary was the oldest class member, but she didn't let her age stop her from being the star student.

After completing her courses at age 117, she was the OLDEST PERSON in history TO LEARN how to READ, WRITE, and DO basic MATH.

Because of her dedication and eagerness to learn at such an old age, Mary was widely celebrated. She was given the city's key and named Chattanooga's Ambassador of Goodwill twice. Leaders worldwide, including President Nixon, congratulated Mary on her achievement.

On her 120th birthday, Mary recited a poem written for her by Norman Eakin to her classmates and teacher called "Four Score and 20 Years-Old."

Mary passed away a year later at 121, becoming the oldest formerly enslaved person to live in America. After her death, her retirement home was named after her. Then, in 1970, a program called the Mary Walker Foundation was formed to increase literacy throughout the city of Chattanooga.

Mary's story is an inspiration to people of all ages. From a formerly enslaved person, she became a top student.

MARY NEVER LET HER AGE, SKIN COLOR, OR GENDER GET IN THE WAY OF HER DESIRE TO LEARN.

Mary's courage to follow her dreams can teach us that no matter how big the obstacles are, it's never too late to learn something new or follow your dreams. Like Mary Hardway Walker, anything is possible if you set your mind to it.

Amelia Earhart

AVIATOR (1897 – 1939)

Amelia Earhart was a world-famous aviator and the first female pilot to fly solo across the Atlantic Ocean.

Use your fear, it CAN TAKE you to the PLACE where you store your COURAGE.

- Amelia Earhart

Born on July 24, 1897, in Atchison, Kansas, Amelia Earhart always sought to take the most adventurous routes through life, even at a young age.

Amelia was just seven years old when she first experimented with flying. She constructed a small aircraft from a wooden box and a makeshift ramp that she attached to the roof of her family's tool shed. Her first flight did not end as she had hoped, as her small, homemade aircraft crashed in the garden shortly after takeoff. Luckily for Amelia, she emerged from the wreckage with only a few minor bumps and bruises.

This minor setback might have discouraged most children from engaging in dangerous activities, but not Amelia. She found the whole experience exhilarating.

When Amelia turned 10, her family moved to Iowa. Her father took young Amelia to the Iowa State Fair, where she saw a real aircraft for the first time. However, Amelia was not interested in flying in the outdated plane she saw at the fair.

As Amelia grew up, she became fond of reading and writing. She chose to study scientific subjects in high school and dreamed of making a success of herself. She even kept a book full of newspaper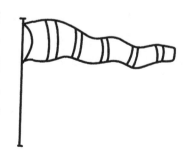

clippings of women who had defied the odds and became successful in careers dominated by men.

As it turned out, Amelia never got the opportunity to complete her studies. In 1917, when visiting her sister in Toronto, Canada, she saw wounded soldiers returning from World War I and decided to train as a nurse with the Red Cross.

A couple of years later, at an air show in California, Amelia had a life-changing moment when she flew for the first time as a passenger. A few minutes into the flight, as the plane soared up through the clouds, she was hooked. From that moment on, she knew she wanted to be a pilot. Shortly after her first flight, Amelia hired one of Iowa's first female pilots, Neta Snook, to become her aviation instructor. Amelia worked tirelessly to afford to pay for flying lessons, balancing several jobs to pursue her dream. She attained her first pilot's license on May 23, 1923.

It became clear that Amelia was no ordinary pilot. Even before she had her pilot's license, she was breaking records. She became the first female pilot to fly at 14,000 feet. But breaking records was not enough to satisfy Amelia's curiosity. By 1928, Amelia had already made a name for herself in the aviation world. That same year, she was asked to accompany Wilmer Stultz on a transatlantic flight from Newfoundland to the United Kingdom. She became the first female to cross the Atlantic in a plane.

Even though she hadn't actually flown the transatlantic flight, this experience earned Amelia worldwide fame and praise. Still, she dreamed of flying a plane across the Atlantic herself.

Her DREAM CAME TRUE in May 1932 when Amelia set off FROM NEWFOUNDLAND on the East Coast of Canada in a SMALL PLANE bound FOR EUROPE.

After battling icy cold winds and mechanical problems, she landed her plane safely in a field in Northern Ireland in just under 15 hours. She was the first woman to fly solo nonstop across the Atlantic Ocean.

The achievement made headlines globally, and Amelia was celebrated as an international hero. But it wasn't long before Amelia was planning her next world-record-breaking feat. She set her sights on flying around the world by following the world's equator. Amelia did extensive planning but had to overcome significant disappointment when her first attempt failed. Her plane was unable to take off from an airfield in Hawaii. However, this setback did not stop Amelia from trying again. Tragically, during Amelia's second attempt, after making it two-thirds of the way, her plane disappeared over the Pacific Ocean, and she was never seen again.

Amelia Earhart never gave up on her dreams. Her story is one of courage and determination to succeed in the face of incredible danger.

AMELIA INSPIRED MILLIONS OF YOUNG WOMEN WHO ASPIRED TO MAKE NAMES FOR THEMSELVES IN MALE-DOMINATED PROFESSIONS.

Her legacy continues to inspire and educate to this day in the form of her aviation company, "The Ninety-Nines," which has championed female pilots for nearly 100 years. Amelia was living proof that overcoming failure and beating the odds when pursuing a dream is something we can all aspire to.

Alfonsina Strada

CYCLIST (1891 – 1959)

Alfonsina Strada was an Italian racing cyclist who competed in the early 1900s. She is the only woman to have competed in one of the three major cycling stage races.

> **÷You NEVER FAIL** *until you* **STOP TRYING.** ÷
>
> – Albert Einstein

Changemakers are often ahead of their time. Such was the case for Italian racing cyclist Alfonsina Strada, who defied the odds and societal norms to become the first female to compete in a grand tour.

Born Alfonsina Morini on March 16, 1891, in the province of Modena, Italy, she was the second of 10 children. Her family was poor, but her dad, Carlo Morini, and her mom, Virginia Marchesini, provided for them as best they could.

Alfonsina earned a tomboy reputation while growing up, pre-ferring to play with her brothers and their friends. Then her dad traded 10 chickens for a battered old bike in 1901. This set off a chain of events forever changing Alfonsina's life.

At just 10 years old, she taught herself to ride and quickly real-ized she had a talent for cycling. However, her parents were not happy. Women were not allowed to vote, let alone com-pete in cycling races, so it was unheard of for girls to want to race and compete. Her mom wanted Alfonsina to settle down, become a seamstress, and stop tearing around the village on her bicycle.

Alfonsina had other ideas. At age 13 in 1904, she secretly took part in her first race. She told her parents that she was going to attend Sunday Mass so as not to raise suspicion. She won that first race, winning a live pig as first prize. Distressed by the ac-tivities of her tomboy daughter, her mom issued an ultimatum. If Alfonsina wanted to continue riding her bike, she must get married and leave home.

This did not deter her in the slightest. She soon married Luigi Strada, a lo-cal metal engraver and mechanic, and the newlyweds moved to Milan. There, Luigi presented Alfonsina with a wed-ding gift — a drop bar racing bike.

Luigi became her trainer and manager as she pedaled into the history books. Alfonsina began to train regularly under the guidance of her husband and soon notched up a series of wins. Eventually, she was invited to compete in the Grand Prix of St Petersburg in Russia in 1909.

Around this time, she also set the world hour record for women, cycling 23.11 miles in 60 minutes on a 44-pound bike — a record that stood for 26 years. Alfonsina went on to win 36 races against men and compete in several big events. But she had her sights set on the biggest race of them all: The Giro d'Italia in 1924.

In a dream come true, ALFONSINA WAS among the 90 riders accepted to compete in the Giro, making her the ONLY WOMAN ever to compete IN A CYCLING GRAND TOUR.

That year, the race was held over 12 stages, covering a distance of 2,245 grueling miles with an average of 187 miles a day. And unlike today, riders had very little support. They had to carry

spare tires and change their own flats. The terrain was treacherous, with high mountain passes and unpaved roads. But none of this deterred Alfonsina.

Young, athletic, and powerful, the 5ft 2inch muscular Alfonsina was determined to complete the race and finished the first four stages well ahead of many other male cyclists. But disaster struck in the eighth stage. Heavy rain and wind caused collapses on the route, making the road slippery. Alfonsina suffered numerous flat tires and a fall that snapped her handlebar in half. She arrived at the finish line out of time and was disqualified.

After a fierce argument with the judges about whether she should be allowed to continue, Alfonsina was officially disqualified. But she had attracted a massive following of fans who had grown fond of the determined and exceptional female rider.

Emilio Colombo, one of the event organizers, saw the public following that Alfonsina had drawn and came up with a solution. The rules stated she could no longer compete, but they didn't say she could not ride. Emilio offered to pay for her board and lodging out of his pocket if she continued riding. And so Alfonsina rode on, cycling into Milan four days later as one of only 31 riders to complete the race. She had outridden 59 other riders through sheer grit and determination. Although not in line for a prize, she was presented with 50,000 lire, raised by public donations, and crowned the "Queen of the Cranks."

Unfortunately, that was the only time she was able to compete in a grand tour. A year later, the event organizers changed the rules, barring female riders from entering the Giro. Undeterred, Alfonsina continued to race in other minor events before retiring to run a small bike shop in Milan.

Alfonsina Strada was a young girl who dreamed of proving she did not have to be held prisoner by other people's expectations or opinions. She led by example and showed that anything is possible with determination and willpower. Despite all the setbacks she faced as a woman during that time, she never let them steer her away from achieving her goals.

LIKE ALFONSINA, YOU CAN **SET GOALS** YOU WANT TO ATTAIN AND **NEVER GIVE UP** ON **ACHIEVING** THEM. **POWER** THROUGH THE **DISAPPOINTMENTS** AND FIND A WAY TO **OVERCOME** THESE **OBSTACLES.**

If Alfonsina could do it all those years ago, so can you.

Over to You

In this chapter, we have met four inspirational women who sold books, learned to read and write at an astounding age, flew un-aided across the Atlantic, and competed in a male-dominated sport before women could even vote. Despite the differences in their achievements, they all took risks, which meant they faced the possibility of failure.

What can we learn from these inspiring women?

Firstly, anything is possible if you set your mind to it and are willing to take risks.

Secondly, failure is a part of success — without it, we would never learn and grow.

Finally, having the right mindset is key to a successful life.

Now it's over to you.

WHAT RISKS ARE YOU WILLING TO TAKE TO ACHIEVE YOUR DREAMS?
AND WHAT MINDSET DO YOU NEED TO HAVE TO BE SUCCESSFUL?

Activity - The Jar of Awesomeness

Sometimes, when things are tough, it can be hard to remember all the good things that have happened in your life.

The Jar of Awesomeness is where you can write down and store all your happy memories and achievements.

WHENEVER YOU'RE FEELING DOWN, YOU CAN TAKE OUT THE JAR AND READ THROUGH ALL THE GREAT THINGS THAT HAVE HAPPENED TO YOU.

To make your own Jar of Awesomeness, find a jar and decorate it however you like. Then, start filling it up with happy memories!

The (Jar) of AWESOMENESS

My Jar of Awesomeness

CHAPTER 5

DREAMING BIG & THINKING OUTSIDE THE BOX

No DREAMER is ever TOO SMALL. No DREAM is ever TOO BiG.

- Turbo Movie

It all STARTS with a DREAM.

A dream to be somebody great, to do something extraordinary, or to make a difference in the world.

When you dare to DREAM BIG, ANYTHING is POSSIBLE.

But what exactly does it mean to dream big and think outside the box?

DREAMING BIG means having the COURAGE TO THINK DIFFERENTLY, be UNIQUE, and imagine SOLUTIONS to problems NO ONE HAS THOUGHT of before.

It means having the confidence to pursue your passions, even if they initially seem impossible.

And it means never giving up, even when things get tough — as these inspirational women have shown….

Billie Jean King

PROFESSIONAL TENNIS PLAYER & ACTIVIST (1943 – PRESENT)

Billie Jean King is one of the greatest tennis players of all time, but her accomplishments go far beyond the tennis court. A vocal advocate for gender equality, she was instrumental in getting women's tennis recognized and accepted as equal to the men's game.

CHAMPIONS
KEEP PLAYING
until they
GET
IT RIGHT.

- Billie Jean King

Billie Jean's story is about much more than just tennis. It is about fighting for what is right and using your platform to make a difference in the world.

Remember, no matter HOW HARD THE FIGHT IS, IT IS ALWAYS WORTH FIGHTING FOR WHAT YOU BELIEVE IN.

Born Billie Jean Moffit on November 22, 1943, in Long Beach, California, she knew from an early age that she wanted to do something with her life and make her mark.

Coming from an athletic family, she loved to play baseball and basketball with her dad and younger brother. But Billie Jean's parents encouraged their daughter to play a more ladylike sport and suggested she take up swimming, golf, or tennis. Golf seemed too slow, and she didn't like to spend time in the water, so she chose tennis.

At age 11, Billie Jean started playing tennis after saving eight dollars for her first racket. From the age of 11 until she was 15, she lived and breathed tennis, practicing whenever she could. In 1959, at age 16, she finished runner-up at the US Girl's National Championships.

Billie Jean was a rising star in the tennis world. In 1961, at age 17, she and her 18-year-old partner Karen Hantze became the youngest duo to win the Wimbledon Doubles title. They repeated the feat the following year.

Five years later, Billie Jean won her first major singles title at Wimbledon. It was the first of many, as she went on to dominate women's tennis for the next 10 years, winning 12 Grand Slam singles titles and 39 in total.

But perhaps Billie Jean's most significant achievements occurred off the tennis court. She was tired of women's tennis being seen as a second-class sport and decided to do something about it.

At that time, the leading men's players earned around $50,000 a year. On the other hand, the best women players only made $5,000. Billie Jean wanted to change that.

She set up the Women's Tennis Association with eight other players. She started organizing women's tournaments with prize money equal to the men's circuit. It was a risky move, but it paid off.

In 1973, the US Open became the first major tennis championship to offer the same prize money to men and women.

But the match dubbed the "Battle of The Sexes" between Billie Jean and Bobby Riggs truly made the world sit up and take notice of her.

RIGGS, A FORMER WORLD NUMBER ONE TENNIS PLAYER WHO WAS NOW IN HIS 50s, BOASTED THAT HE COULD BEAT ANY WOMAN.

Billie Jean took him up on his challenge.

The match was televised worldwide, and 90 million people tuned in to watch.

BILLIE JEAN WON, AND IN DOING SO, PROVED THAT WOMEN COULD COMPETE WITH MEN ON A LEVEL PLAYING FIELD.

It was a massive moment for tennis and women's sports in general.

Following her win over Riggs, Billie Jean continued to fight for gender equality in sports. She founded the Women's Sports Foundation, which is dedicated to advancing the lives of women and girls through sports and physical activity.

Today, Billie Jean is still involved in campaigning for gender equality and women's rights. She is also a keen tennis player and coach.

Billie Jean King is a true pioneer and an inspiration to anyone, regardless of gender, who wants to achieve success in their field.

EVEN WHEN THE ODDS ARE AGAINST YOU, HARD WORK, DEDICATION, AND A NEVER-GIVE-UP ATTITUDE ARE THE KEYS TO ACHIEVING YOUR DREAMS.

Jazz Jennings

YOUTUBE PERSONALITY & LGBTQ ACTIVIST (2000 – PRESENT)

Jazz Jennings is a trans YouTuber and LGBTQ activist who uses her platform to speak out for the safety and acceptance of trans kids.

ANYTHING is **possible** with **SUNSHINE** and a **LITTLE PINK.**

- Jazz Jennings

Jazz Jennings was born on October 6, 2000, in Southern Florida. Although she was born male, she was already questioning her gender identity at two years old. Over the next few years, she continued to feel like she was a girl born into the wrong body. After being diagnosed with gender identity disorder, Jazz spent most of her time at home dressed as a girl while appearing publicly as a boy. Eventually growing tired of hiding, Jazz wore a one-piece swimsuit on her fifth birthday and officially announced to her friends that she was a girl.

While Jazz's family and close friends supported her identity, her parents feared she might be subjected to transphobia. Jazz's identity made her a vulnerable target for bullying and discrimination. She and her family chose to stay private for Jazz's safety. But when schools refused to allow Jazz to enroll as a girl, her family decided to speak out about her treatment.

In 2007, at just six years old, Jazz gave an interview on the TV show "20/20" with Barbara Walters and quickly became a spokesperson for the transgender community. At a time when there were very few stories about trans kids, Jazz's experience gained enormous attention for the visibility she was bringing to trans youths.

Together with her family, six-year-old Jazz described what her journey had been like so far. She explained how she was grow-ing her hair out, wearing dresses like other girls, and using she/her pronouns at school. Her parents also added that before Jazz came out, her mental health suffered due to being unable to express her true self.

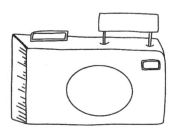

Jazz and her family hoped SHARING their STORY might HELP other PARENTS SUPPORT their TRANS KIDS.

Shortly after her interview on 20/20, Jazz and her parents founded the Transkids Purple Rainbows Foundation, which provides support and resources for trans youth.

Her first TV appearance was quickly followed by several others, including interviews with Oprah Winfrey and Rosie O'Donnell. Her personal YouTube account also became a source of inspiration for trans audiences. Her posts included a vlog series of her day-to-day life called I Am Jazz. I Am Jazz later became a TLC reality TV show in 2015. It followed Jazz and her family as they navigated life through a transgender lens.

At 11 years old, Jazz began her medical transition by taking hormone blockers, which temporarily paused the masculinization of her body. She later continued the process by taking estrogen in high school. Then finally, at 18, Jazz got the gender confirmation surgery she had always wanted.

Fast forward a few years, and Jazz was named one of the "25 Most Influential Teenagers of 2014" by Time Magazine. She was accepted into Harvard University, published two books, and was named a Human Rights Campaign Youth Ambassador.

Throughout Jazz's journey, she never let societal expectations limit her dreams. She stayed true to who she was and forged a path for other trans youth worldwide to be themselves. Instead of hiding, Jazz was determined to build a life for herself and use her platform to make a difference in the world.

SHE IS A REMINDER THAT NO MATTER WHO YOU ARE OR WHERE YOU COME FROM, YOU CAN ACHIEVE ANYTHING YOU WANT.

We can follow in Jazz's footsteps by having the courage to be ourselves and use our voices to speak up for those who remain silenced.

Dame Anita Roddick

FOUNDER OF THE BODY SHOP (1976 – 2007)

Anita Roddick was a UK activist, an environmentalist, and founder of The Body Shop. A pioneer in the natural cosmetics industry, she was one of the first to promote eco-friendly and ethically produced products.

Be DARING,
be FIRST,
be DIFFERENT,
be JUST.

- Anita Roddick

Anita Roddick had modest goals when she opened The Body Shop in Brighton, UK, in 1976. She wanted to supply quality beauty products, advertise them honestly, and support her daughter while her husband was away in South America. Soon, however, she started dreaming bigger, and her business quickly expanded.

Within 15 years, her single store had grown into 700 Body Shop locations worldwide. Fast-forward another 13 years, her business catered to 77 million customers at 1,980 stores globally. Anita was one of England's most successful entrepreneurs, but she was not only a businesswoman — she was also someone who campaigned for both environmental and human rights causes throughout her life.

These causes were not a side project but a significant part of The Body Shop's brand. Anita believed business was not just about money but also about being a force for good in the world.

Anita was born in October 1942 in Sussex, England. When she was young, her mother gave her some advice that stayed with her for life:

"WHATEVER YOU DO, BE DIFFERENT."

When The Body Shop first opened, it differed from the typical beauty stores of the time. It was a small, humble, green shop without any of the usual shiny, fancy décors that most beauty shops had.

ANITA WAS A PIONEER, FOCUSING ON SIMPLE PRODUCTS MADE FROM NATURAL INGREDIENTS THAT WERE NOT TESTED ON ANIMALS.

These products had plain packaging, with bottles that could be refilled.

Rather than producing adverts like most other beauty companies, showing only glamorous, slim models, The Body Shop wanted women to feel comfortable in their bodies. This led Anita to market to ordinary people and celebrate women of all body types, races, and cultures. "Beauty is an outward expression of everything you like about yourself," was her message.

Many of Anita's business ideas are now common, but they didn't exist when she started out. She was ahead of her time in promoting sustainable, cruelty-free, ethically sourced ingredients and products, paving the way for other beauty companies to do the same.

In 1986, Anita teamed up with the global environmental organization Greenpeace, working with them on a Save the Whales campaign. Anita used plant-based jojoba oil in her products rather than whale oil, a common ingredient at the time. She advocated for the rest of the beauty industry to do the same.

This was the beginning of years of work for a range of causes. Equally devoted to making life better for humans and animals, Anita started a community fair trade program in 1987 to obtain natural ingredients from around the world while benefiting the communities these ingredients came from rather than exploiting them.

She founded Children on the Edge (COTE) in 1990 to help children in orphanages and those who faced challenges, such as disabilities, natural disasters, wars, and diseases like HIV/Aids. Anita was inspired to start COTE after witnessing the overcrowded conditions in orphanages in Romania.

Anita was also involved with many other environmental and human rights campaigns. She did not believe that people should be silent about cruelty and injustice. She thought that The Body Shop, and other businesses, could play a key role in making the world a better place.

"BUSINESS SHAPES THE WORLD. IT IS CAPABLE OF CHANGING SOCIETY IN ALMOST ANY WAY YOU CAN IMAGINE," SHE ONCE SAID.

In 2003, Anita was knighted by Queen Elizabeth II. This gave her the official title of Dame Commander of the Order of the British Empire, but to most people, she was better known by her nickname, the "Queen of Green."

Sadly, Dame Anita passed away in 2007 at age 64. She ensured her activism and charitable work would continue, making good on a promise and donating her entire £51 million fortune to charity.

Anita Roddick was a true original. She didn't just sell lotions and potions — she changed how business was done. She showed the world that it is possible to be successful and do good simultaneously.

DREAM BIG, THINK OUTSIDE THE BOX, AND DON'T BE AFRAID TO BE DIFFERENT.

That's what Anita Roddick taught us.

SO GO OUT THERE AND MAKE YOUR MARK ON THE WORLD. AND ASK YOURSELF THIS QUESTION: "WHAT WILL MY LEGACY BE?"

Kalpana Chawla

ASTRONAUT (1962 – 2003)

Kalpana Chawla was an Indian-born American astronaut and mechanical engineer who was the first Indian American woman to go to space.

The path from DREAMS *to* SUCCESS *does* exist.

— Kalpana Chawla

You might have heard people say, "Reach for the stars!" This is a phrase that means to aspire to something great, no matter how impossible it might seem.

FOR KALPANA CHAWLA, REACHING FOR THE STARS WAS NOT JUST A FIGURE OF SPEECH – IT WAS HER LITERAL AMBITION.

And she achieved it, becoming the first Indian American woman in space.

Born Montu Chawla in March 1962 in Karnal, India, she was the youngest of four children in a family where hard work was encouraged. Growing up in India in the 1960s was not easy for girls, as they were expected to be docile and obedient and not strive for higher education. But Kalpana's mom came from an educated family and wanted more for her daughters.

Even as a child, Montu began to show her independence. She even selected her own name when she started kindergarten!

 Her parents had not gotten around to a formal naming ceremony and instead used the nickname "Montu." But when the kindergarten principal asked her what name she would like to be called, without hesitation, she said: "Kalpana," which means "idea" or "imagination" in Hindi.

Growing up, Kalpana would often go up onto the roof of the house in summer with her family and watch the night sky, dreaming of one day venturing into space. Another favorite pastime of hers was to watch airplanes take off and land at the nearby Karnal Aviation Club, waving to the pilots as they flew overhead. Then, one day, no longer content to stand and wave at the airplanes, Kalpana persuaded her dad to let her take her first trip in a two-seat cabin monoplane. From that day forward, flying became her inspiration.

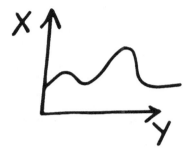

By 10th grade, when she was 12 years old, Kalpana had made up her mind: She wanted to become a flight engineer and wasn't going to let anything stand in her way. After completing her pre-university and pre-engineering courses, she enrolled in Punjab Engineering College.

DESPITE ALL THE BARRIERS SHE HAD FACED, AT 20 YEARS OLD, KALPANA BECAME THE FIRST WOMAN AT HER COLLEGE TO RECEIVE AN ENGINEERING DEGREE.

During this time, she realized she would require more practical hands-on experience. Unfortunately, her home country India was still years away from having serious space initiatives of its own. So, Kalpana applied for and got accepted into the University of Texas in the US to pursue a master of science degree in aerospace engineering.

When she was not studying, Kalpana and her husband Jean would be at the local airfield learning how to fly. Despite her short stature, Kalpana was not put off. Instead, she used extra cushions to reach the controls in the plane. She quickly became a certified flight instructor for airplanes, gliders, and commercial pilots.

After obtaining her master's degree in 1984, Kalpana earned a second master's degree in 1986 and a Ph.D. in aerospace engineering in 1988.

For the next couple of years, Kalpana never lost sight of her goal as she worked towards becoming an astronaut. In 1991, she became a US citizen. She was accepted as an astronaut candidate at the NASA (National Aeronautics and Space Administration) Astronaut Corps. At age 35, she achieved her goal when, in November 1997, she officially became the first Indian-born woman in space, flying aboard the space shuttle Columbia. Kalpana had done it. All those years of studying and all the sacrifices she'd made had paid off.

But after getting her first taste of space, she wanted more. In 2003, at age 40, she was chosen for her second flight on Columbia's ill-fated 28th mission. Less than a month later, disaster struck when the shuttle disintegrated over Texas during re-entry into earth's atmosphere, killing all seven crew members.

But Kalpana's legacy lives on.

HER HARD WORK AND DETERMINATION AS SHE CHIPPED AWAY AT HER GOALS HAVE INSPIRED MANY OTHER YOUNG WOMEN TO PURSUE THEIR DREAMS, NO MATTER HOW OUT OF REACH THEY MAY SEEM.

Kalpana dreamed big. Even in the face of adversity, she persevered and never lost focus on the steps she needed to take to achieve her goals.

Just like Kalpana, you can achieve the impossible if you set your mind to it.

BELIEVE IN SOMETHING SINCERELY AND MAKE IT YOURS THROUGH HARD WORK, DETERMINATION, AND PERSEVERANCE.

Remember, you can achieve the impossible by reaching beyond what you believe is possible.

Over to You

To ACHIEVE GREAT THINGS IN LIFE, YOU HAVE TO DREAM BIG.

But everyone's dreams are different. Some people dream of becoming famous singers or actors, while others dream of becoming astronauts or politicians.

It is essential to find what you're passionate about and go after it with everything you've got.

Kalpana Chawla was passionate about space exploration. She didn't let anything stop her from achieving her dream of becoming an astronaut.

Anita Roddick dreamed of starting her own ethical business that did things differently. She did just that with The Body Shop.

THE POINT IS THAT YOUR UNIQUENESS IS YOUR SUPERPOWER. IT'S WHAT MAKES YOU SPECIAL, AND IT'S WHAT WILL HELP YOU ACHIEVE YOUR DREAMS.

Activity - Think Outside the Box

As we have already seen, successful people approach problems creatively. They don't just accept things as they are but instead look for innovative solutions.

Like anything else, thinking outside the box is a skill that can be learned.

The MORE you PRACTICE CREATIVITY, the EASIER it BECOMES.

Here's a fun activity to help you get started.

Instructions:

1. Take a look at the picture on the next page. It's incomplete — some pieces are missing.

2. Your task is to use your imagination to finish the picture. Think outside the box and be creative!

3. What did you come up with? What story does your picture tell?

THINK
OUTSIDE
the box

Complete the picture... it is **NOT** a balloon...

Go get 'em...

If you CAN DREAM IT, you CAN ACHIEVE IT.

Whatever you want to be — wherever you want to go in life — don't let anyone stop you. Just keep going.

Things won't always be easy; you'll have tough times and make mistakes. But if you don't give up and always keep pushing forward, you will achieve anything you set your mind to.

So, what are you waiting for? Go out there and make your dreams come true!

IT'S TIME TO ACHIEVE SOMETHING GREAT.

NOTHING is IMPOSSIBLE,

the word itself says

'I'M POSSIBLE!'

- Audrey Hepburn

Now it's your turn... draw your portrait:

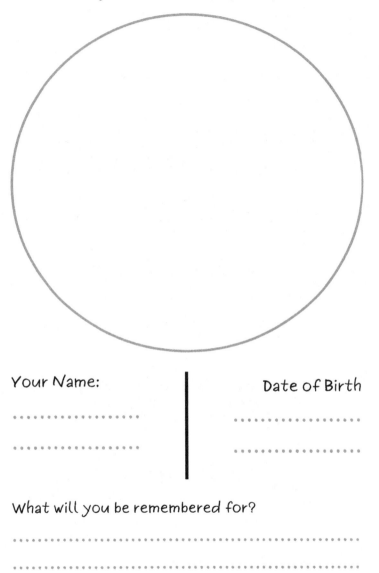

Your Name: | Date of Birth

. . . .

. . . .

What will you be remembered for?

. . . .

. . . .

What's your favorite quote? Write it down here:

Write your story:

Be **STRONG,**

be **FEARLESS,**

be **BEAUTIFUL.**

And believe that

ANYTHING IS

POSSIBLE.

- Misty Copeland

THANKS
FOR READING OUR
BOOK!

We really hope that you and your child are inspired by the incredible women featured in this book.

We would be so grateful if you could take a few seconds to leave an honest review or a star rating on Amazon. (A star rating takes just a couple of clicks).

Your review also helps other parents discover this book, and it might help their tween children on their journeys. Plus, it will also be good Karma for you.

To leave a review

SCAN
HERE

LIKED THIS?
WE THINK YOU'LL
LOVE THIS!

"I wish I had this book when I was younger."

-Amazon Customer

Get your copy today.

SCAN HERE

Made in United States
North Haven, CT
21 December 2022

29946692R00104